USING THIS BOOK

*Children learn to read by **reading**, but they need help to begin with.*

When you have read the story on the left-hand pages aloud to the child, go back to the beginning of the book and look at the pictures together.

Encourage children to read the sentences under the pictures. If they don't know a word, give them a chance to 'guess' what it is from the illustrations, before telling them.

There are more suggestions for helping children to learn to read in the *Parent/Teacher* booklet.

British Library Cataloguing in Publication Data
McCullagh, Sheila K.
    Magic balloons. — (Puddle Lane. Stage 2; v.10)
    1. Readers — 1950-
    I. Title   II. Dillow, John   III. Series
    428.6   PE1119
    ISBN 0-7214-0972-5

First edition

Published by Ladybird Books Ltd Loughborough Leicestershire UK
Ladybird Books Inc Lewiston Maine 04240 USA

Printed in England

Magic balloons

written by SHEILA McCULLAGH
illustrated by JOHN DILLOW

This book belongs to:

Ladybird Books

The Magician lived in an attic room
in the old house in Puddle Lane.
He didn't often go down
into the lane, but he had
a magic puddle of water
on the floor of his room.
When he looked into the puddle,
and said the right spell,
the water in the magic puddle
became as clear as glass.
He could look into it and
see what was happening
down below in Puddle Lane.

the Magician

One day, the Magician looked into
his magic puddle of water,
and saw old Mr Gotobed
sitting outside his house
in Puddle Lane.
Mr Gotobed was sitting
in the sunshine, and
he was fast asleep.

The Magician looked
into the magic water.

Peter Puffle came charging
up the lane, riding his wagon.
He had a tin trumpet in his hand,
and he blew the trumpet loudly
in Mr Gotobed's ear
as he went by.
Mr Gotobed woke up with a start,
but before he could say anything,
Peter had turned his wagon around,
and charged off down the lane.
"I wish that boy would play
somewhere else!" said Mr Gotobed.
He got up, and went into
his house, shaking his head.

Peter Puffle
came up the lane.
Mr Gotobed woke up.

Sarah and Davy
came through the gates,
out of the garden.
They were pulling their music box along
on an old cart they had made.
Peter came rushing back up the lane
on his wagon.
"Hello, Peter," said Davy.
"Let's have a blow on that trumpet."

"Get one for yourself. This one's mine,"
said Peter.
He turned the wagon round,
and went off down the lane.

Sarah and Davy
met Peter Puffle.

"Never mind, Davy," said Sarah.
"Our music box is much better
than his silly trumpet."
She gave the cart a pull,
but as it moved forward
a wheel fell off.

Sarah pulled the cart.

"That's done it," said Sarah.
"We'll have to mend it."
They lifted the magic music box
out of the cart, and
set it down on the ground.
Then they turned the cart
on one side, to look at
the wheel.

Sarah and Davy
took the box
out of the cart.

They were just trying to fix
the wheel on again, when
Peter Puffle came rushing back,
riding his wagon.
He stopped to watch them.
"Has that old thing broken down
again?" he said.

"Lend us your wagon, Peter,"
said Sarah. "Then we can
take the music box home,
and come back for the cart."

Peter came back
up the lane.
He stopped to look
at Sarah and Davy.

"You can't have it," said Peter.
"**I** want it."

"It will only be for a few minutes,
Peter," said Davy. "Just while
we take the music box home."

"It's **my** wagon, and
I'm playing with it," said Peter.
And he went off down the lane.
Davy and Sarah picked up
the music box, and
carried it home between them.

Peter Puffle went
down the lane.
Sarah and Davy
picked up the box.

The Magician watched
everything in the magic puddle of water.
"I think I'll go down
into Puddle Lane,"
he said to himself.
"I'll make a little magic.
I'll go down and see Peter Puffle."
He muttered a spell, and
snapped his fingers.

The Magician said,
"I will make
a little magic."

In a flash, the Magician vanished,
and an old man stood there
with a bunch of balloons in his hand.
The Magician laughed softly
to himself, and went out
of the door of his attic room,
down the stairs and
through the garden, and
out into Puddle Lane.

The Magician vanished,
and an old man was there,
with balloons in his hand.

Peter Puffle came charging
up the lane in his wagon.
He saw the Magician, and stopped.
"Are you selling those balloons?"
he asked. "I'll have them."

"How many do you want?"
asked the Magician.

"I want them all," said Peter.

"Aren't there other children
in Puddle Lane, who'd like one?"
asked the Magician.

"Yes," said Peter. "But
I'm here first. I'll buy them all."
He pulled out some money, and
the Magician gave him
the bunch of balloons.

The Magician
gave the balloons
to Peter Puffle.

As soon as Peter took hold
of the bunch of balloons,
he shot up into the air.
He hung there, as high
as the roofs of the houses,
and he clung to the balloons
as hard as he could.
"Help!" cried Peter.
"Help! Get me down!"

The balloons took
Peter Puffle up
to the roofs
of the houses.

Sarah and Davy came running
out of their house.
"Peter!" cried Sarah. "Come down!"
Hari and Gita looked out
of their door.

"We'll get a ladder," cried Hari.

"Peter!" cried Sarah.
"Come down!"

"We will get a ladder,"
cried Hari.

"There's no need for a ladder,"
said the Magician.
"Let go of the balloons one by one.
Don't let them all go at once.
If you let them go
one at a time,
you will come down slowly."

"Let the balloons go,
one by one,"
said the Magician.

Peter let a balloon go, and
he came down a little way
towards the ground.
The balloon floated down,
and Sarah caught it.

Peter let a balloon go.
He came down
a little way.

"Now let the next one go,"
said the Magician.
Peter let another balloon go,
and then another.
He dropped down until
he could see in the top windows
of the houses.
The balloons floated down
into Puddle Lane.
Gita caught one, and
Hari caught the other one.

Peter let a balloon go.
He came down
a little way.

"One more," said the Magician.
Peter let one more balloon go,
and dropped down still further.
The balloon floated down,
and Davy caught it.
"Now let all the others go,"
said the Magician.
Peter let the balloons go,
and dropped safely to the ground.
The balloons floated away,
up and over the roofs
of the houses.

"Let all the balloons go,"
said the Magician.

"Are you all right, Peter?"
asked Davy.

"I think so," said Peter.

"Here's your balloon," said Gita,
holding it out to him.

"You can have it," said Peter.
"I don't want it.
I don't want any of them.
You can keep them all."
He ran off down the lane.

"Here is your balloon,
Peter," said Gita.
"You can have it,"
said Peter.

Gita turned to the Magician.
"What shall we do
with the balloons?" she asked.

"Play with them," said the Magician.
"They're yours.
Peter gave them to you."
He went back up the lane
to his house, laughing softly
to himself.

The Magician went
back to his house.

The children stood watching him,
until he went into the garden.
"Was he the Magician?"
asked Gita.

"He must have been," said Hari.
"They must be **magic** balloons."

"They seem all right now,"
said Davy.

"Let's go and mend our cart,"
said Sarah. "And then
we can play with the balloons."
The four children went off
up the lane together,
to mend the old cart.

Sarah and Davy,
Hari and Gita
went up the lane
with the balloons.

Have you read these stories about the Magician?

from The Magician's party

*from
Tessa in
Puddle Lane*

from Tim Catchamouse